OUTLAWS OF THE AMERICAN WEST

OUTLAWS

OF
THE

AMERICAN
WEST

BY D. J. HERDA

THE MILLBROOK PRESS
BROOKFIELD, CONNECTICUT

Cover photo courtesy of
Denver Public Library, Western History Collections

Photos courtesy of Archive Photos: p. 6; Bettman: pp. 8, 9,
13 (top), 39, 52; Kansas State Historical Society, Topeka: pp. 11,
15, 21 (bottom); New York Public Library Picture Collection:
p. 13 (bottom); Amon Carter Museum, Fort Worth, Texas: p.
14 ("In Without Knocking" by Charles M. Russell); Denver
Public Library, Western History Collections: pp. 17, 45, 48;
Photofest: pp. 18, 32, 46, 58; Minnesota Historical Society:
pp. 21 (top, photo: Sumner Studio, Northfield, Minn.), 27
(photo: Sumner Gallery), 28; North Wind Picture Archives:
pp. 25, 49; Western History Collections, University of Okla-
homa: p. 31; Museum of New Mexico: pp. 35, 43 (right);
The Beinecke Rare Book and Manuscript Library, Yale
University: p. 43 (left); Pinkerton Security and Investiga-
tion Services, Pinkerton's Inc., Encino, Calif., 91436: p.
55 (reprinted with permission).

Library of Congress Cataloging-in-Publication Data
Herda, D.J., 1948–
Outlaws of the American West / by D. J. Herda.
p.   cm.
Includes bibliographical references (p.) and index.
Summary: Examines the most famous outlaws of the
American West, recounting their exploits and con-
sidering the factors that contributed to their rise.
ISBN 1-56294-449-5
1. Outlaws—West (U.S.)—History—Juvenile literature.
2. West (U.S)—History—1848–1860—Juvenile literature.
3. West (U.S.)—History—1860–1890—Juvenile literature.
F596.H39 1995 978'.02'0922—dc20 94-11296 CIP AC

Published by The Millbrook Press, Inc.
2 Old New Milford Road, Brookfield, Connecticut 06804

CONTENTS

FOREWORD

Outlaws of the American West. They have been glorified in movies, fictionalized on television, glamorized in novels—and for good reason. Between 1840 and 1900, some of the most remarkable characters in American history lived west of the Mississippi River. This was the age of bank robbers, rail raiders, and gunslingers.

But was outlawry in the American West really the way it has been shown in the media?

"It wasn't nothin' like that a'tall," recalled Jonathan Bedford, who had been a child of six when—in 1859—his family packed up the wagon and moved west from Kansas along the Santa Fe Trail, eventually settling in present-day north central Colorado. Bedford witnessed at firsthand the realities of everyday life in the American West: long days of toiling under the hot sun, learning to read and write in a one-room log cabin, and trying to beat the frost and snow to the sparse crops of hay and oats the family raised for livestock.[1]

Throughout his life, Bedford never once came across a murderer, bank robber, or gunslinger. He never encountered a cattle rustler or train robber. He never even saw a horse thief. So rare were such characters that most Westerners had to read about them in the weekly news-

The truth about the American West was stretched not only in newspapers and dime novels, but in publications that combined the two. This one served up tall tales of the West on a weekly basis.

paper or in the popular novels—called dime novels or "penny dreadfuls"—of the day.

Still, the outlaws of legend *were* part of the American West. A special combination of factors allowed these few, much-mythologized men to exist.

GOLD!

On January 24, 1848, a group of prospectors working the South Fork of California's American River struck gold near a sawmill owned by John Sutter. Word of the strike traveled quickly, and by December 5, gold fever had spread throughout the country. More than 80,000 people swarmed to California in 1849 alone. The Mexicans who had been living there soon became the minority as the promise of fast wealth brought thousands of "Forty-niners," as those who rushed to California from the East in 1849 were called.

Nearly a decade later, in 1858, news—greatly exaggerated—of another strike near present-day Denver, Colorado, reached the eastern United States. Tens of thousands of Americans struck by gold fever swarmed into the mining camps hastily thrown up at Aurora, Central City, Golden, Boulder, and Cripple Creek.

Although a few of these prospectors struck enormous wealth in the rivers and mountains of Colorado and California, most never found more than a few nuggets—barely enough to keep them in beans and pork. Those who did found something else they never bargained for—a class of cheaters, swindlers, robbers, and murderers intent upon helping themselves to the vast new riches of their fellow Americans. These were the West's infamous outlaws.

Searching for gold was tedious and only on rare occasions productive work. Here a California miner pours gravel mixed with water into a "cradle," which another miner uses to sift the mixture in the hope of finding a few precious grains.

THE CIVIL WAR

With the outbreak of the Civil War in 1861, the massive flow of people into the West slowed. Then, in 1862, Congress passed the Homestead Act. This act granted 160 acres (65 hectares) of land to anyone twenty-one years of age or older. A homesteader had to build a shelter on the land, live there for five years, and fulfill a few other requirements. After that, the homesteader received legal title to the land.

Although eastern farmers were skeptical of the quality of the free land, the Homestead Act once again brought people to the West. Some were northerners who helped increase the Union presence in the West. Others were southerners who, like the notorious James brothers, Frank and Jesse, were sympathetic to the Confederate cause and angry that the West was filling up with Yankees. At least in the case of the James brothers, the conflicts that had fueled the Civil War also fueled—or perhaps provided an excuse for—criminal activity.

EAST MEETS WEST

The West played a key role throughout the war, with both Union and Confederacy competing to control mining regions and supply routes. Recognizing the importance of developing the area, President Abraham Lincoln in 1862 authorized construction of the transcontinental railroad. That year the Central Pacific began laying tracks in Sacramento, California, while the Union Pacific started in Omaha, Nebraska. The plan was to have the tracks meet in between.

On May 10, 1869, the Union and Central Pacific railroads met at a place called Promontory Point in Utah. There, railroad officials and politicians celebrated the completion of the nation's first transcontinental, or cross-country, railroad by driving a golden spike into the last railroad tie.

Homesteaders had a difficult life, often farming large areas of land with little help and meager tools. This photo shows a homesteader family on its farm.

Now, at last, the West was opened to increased settlement. The railroads making the cross-country trip carried men, women, and children, as well as the goods and supplies demanded by a booming population. They carried money, too—gold, cash, and bonds—for the banks that had sprung up throughout the West, making trains the ideal target for outlaws.

MOVE 'EM OUT

As the railroads steadily worked their way west, an old industry was suddenly reborn—cattle ranching. Ranchers had been raising cattle in southern Texas since early Spanish explorers introduced longhorns and other types of cattle to the area in the 1700s. Now the ranchers realized that, instead of selling their cattle locally for three or four dollars a head, they could sell them for ten to twenty times as much to buyers in the East. So once each year, after the cattle had grown fat grazing the lush grasslands from Texas north to Montana, they were rounded up and herded to a railhead, where they were loaded onto trains for the trip east.

Yet the cattle drives were not without their hardships. Many cattle were lost to disease and predators along the way. Others fell prey to the greedy hands of cattle rustlers, who would swoop down on a herd of several thousand head, separate out a few hundred, and race the main herd to the railhead, where they would sell the stolen cattle as their own.

A NEW CODE OF JUSTICE

As outlawry spread throughout the West, a new code of justice was born. The West's first agents of law and order were soldiers and militiamen. In a region where one lawman was often responsible for policing up to several hundred miles of territory, it became clear that help was needed. This help came in the form of the posse—a group of local citizens deputized to act as lawmen. Most posses were given free rein to scour the territory for lawbreakers.

With few courts and even fewer judges available, justice on the plains often came swiftly and firmly. People accused of being horse thieves, swindlers, or murderers were apprehended, tried, convicted, and hanged from a nearby tree, often within minutes of their arrest.

Left: The Central Pacific relied heavily on Chinese and European immigrants to build its portion of the transcontinental railroad. Here laborers of many types join in the hard work of running track through solid rock. Below: Cowboys at breakfast during a cattle drive. Like outlaws, cowboys led lives that were far less glamorous than Hollywood or the printed page made them out to be: Cattle drives were long, exhausting, and dangerous affairs.

This painting shows the West's outlaws as many people imagine them: lawless wild men whooping and shooting their way to fame and fortune.

Reality was, however, far more grim: This photo shows what happened when members of two Kansas families—fighting over water rights—took the law into their own hands.

This new form of vigilante justice placed tremendous power in the hands of a few poorly trained citizens. With no other law than the badges on their chest and the guns at their sides, some posse members slipped across the line between law enforcer and lawbreaker.

But the lawbreakers and the outlaws, the bandits and the thieves, were few and far between in the wide open spaces of the American

West. By far, the vast majority of Americans in the West were decent, honest, law-abiding citizens.

Still, the few who were not are those we remember best. There are many reasons why these men have been glorified and celebrated. Some say that, during the nineteenth century, newspaper editors and dime novelists portrayed outlaws as daring thrill-seekers rather than as vicious criminals to give their stories a wide appeal and increase sales. Others add that show business has continued this practice in our own time with romanticized movie versions of outlaws' lives.

Are such makeovers of men who murdered, cheated, lied, and stole merely harmless entertainment? Or do they distract us from the fact that their crimes and violence ruined lives, destroyed communities, and ultimately threatened freedom? These are questions to ponder as you read these accounts of the James brothers, Billy the Kid, and Butch Cassidy and the Wild Bunch—the outlaws of the American West.

WANTED

FRANK & JESSE
JAMES

This scene from the 1951 movie "Jesse James" shows the James Gang blasting its way out of the First National Bank.

On September 7, 1876, five men on horseback rode into the town of Northfield, Minnesota, firing their pistols in the air and shouting wildly. As the townspeople fled for cover, three of the men, wearing wide-brimmed hats and long cotton dusters, hopped off their horses. Flashing their pistols, they burst through the doors of the First National Bank.

Once inside, the three outlaws leaped over the cashier's counter and ordered teller Joseph Heywood and two co-workers to put up their hands. Heywood instinctively dashed for the open vault, but the outlaws reached it first. One of the desperadoes, a twenty-nine-year-old Missourian with steel-gray eyes and a closely cropped beard, spied the closed safe inside the vault and demanded that Heywood open it. It was the first time the teller had ever looked down the barrel of a gun. The gun belonged to Jesse James.

Trembling uncontrollably, Heywood stammered: "It . . . it has a time lock. It can't be opened."[1]

Whether Heywood was telling the truth is not clear. What historians *are* certain of, however, is that James and his gang of hardened outlaws did not leave Northfield with any money that day. And some of the gang did not live to leave at all.

AN EARLY VOW

Jesse Woodson James was born on September 5, 1847, on a farm near Kearney, Missouri. The younger of two brothers, Jesse was a rowdy, impulsive youth constantly seeking adventure. His elder brother, Alexander Franklin James ("Frank" for short) was born on January 10, 1843. His father, Robert, was a Baptist preacher, and his mother, Zerelda Cole Mimms, a hard-working Kentucky farm woman.

When the Civil War broke out in 1861, the James brothers—like many Missourians who believed that slavery should remain legal—sided with the Confederacy. Within two years, both Frank and Jesse, then teenagers, joined a band of Confederate outlaws—often called bushwhackers—led by Colonel William Clarke Quantrill. In time, the notorious William "Bloody Bill" Anderson joined the band. In 1863 they attacked and looted the Union town of Lawrence, Kansas, to secure goods and money for their cause. On the orders of Quantrill—noted for his viciousness—the band destroyed much of the community and killed all the male inhabitants they could find, about 150 of them, both young and old.

In return, a group of Union soldiers swept across the plains to the James farm. The soldiers looted the family's buildings, set fire to their crops, and freed the slaves. When Jesse showed up and tried to stop the soldiers, he was beaten nearly to death.

While recovering from his injuries, Jesse, only seventeen years old, vowed to get revenge. By then, the younger of the two James brothers had become an expert horseman, a status he never achieved as a marksman. As soon as he recovered, he rode off to join brother Frank and Cole Younger, a cousin of the James family and a notorious gunman, to fight the Union forces. Riding once again under the command of Quantrill, they sacked Union towns and frustrated Northern forces wherever they went.

The real Frank and Jesse James.

Below: Quantrill's raiders were merciless in their sack of Lawrence, Kansas, as this engraving shows. They terrorized women and children and burned buildings. Some historians have since questioned Jesse James's role in the raid, claiming he wasn't present.

As the bloodiest war in American history raged on, the James brothers' fame spread. Union soldiers now regularly raided the family farm, hoping to catch Frank and Jesse there—but to no avail.

In 1865, with the war nearly ended, the U.S. government issued a general amnesty for all vigilante groups that had committed crimes in the name of the Confederacy. If the roving bands would set down their guns and return to their homes, the amnesty promised, all charges against them would be dropped.

Seeing a chance to return to life on the farm without paying for his crimes, Jesse was eager to take advantage of the offer. He led a small band of men toward Lexington, Missouri, to surrender their guns. The band included Frank James and Cole Younger. On the way, they were attacked by a company of Union troops. Jesse was knocked off his horse by a bullet that pierced his left lung.

LIFE OUTSIDE THE LAW

Narrowly escaping with their lives, Frank and Jesse returned to the family farm in Missouri. But they soon discovered that farm life was nowhere nearly as exciting as life on the run, so on February 13, 1866, Frank and Jesse buckled up their gun belts and headed off to Liberty, a neighboring town. With them were eight other men, including Cole Younger. When they reached Liberty, Frank and Cole went into the Clay County Savings Bank, while the others held the horses outside.

As Frank approached William and Greenup Bird, a father and son who worked at the bank as cashiers, he told them, "If you make any noise, you will be shot."[2] He then instructed the two bankers to place in an empty wheat sack all of the money from behind the teller's cage and within the vault. The two robbers emerged from the bank minutes later with more than $60,000 in gold and bonds.

As the ten men rode slowly out of town, they passed George Wymore, who was crossing the town square. Wymore stopped and stared at one of the outlaws as though he knew him. The rider slowed his horse to a stop and wheeled around in his saddle, then drew his pistol and fired three deadly shots into the startled man. The other gang members began firing wildly into the air as the band sped down the main street and out of town.

The sheriff quickly formed a posse and set out in pursuit of the robbers, but the gang by then had crossed the Missouri River and disappeared in a raging snowstorm. Inside of a few fateful minutes, the James brothers had committed a bank robbery and a murder. News of the bold attack on the Liberty Bank went out over chattering telegraph wires almost immediately.

Eight months after the Liberty robbery, the James Gang struck again. This time they robbed the Mitchell Bank in Lexington of $2,000—a far cry from the $100,000 Frank had expected to get. The gang members were disappointed, but it would not be the last disappointment they would have.

On March 2, 1867, the James Gang rode up to the local bank in Savanna, Missouri. Once inside, Jesse and Frank asked to speak to the bank president. When Judge John McClain stepped out of his office, the gangsters pulled their guns and pointed them at his head. They demanded the keys to the vault. McClain refused, and Jesse allegedly shot him in the chest. The two brothers ran from the bank, making their getaway into the outlying hills.

Still hurting over their second unsuccessful robbery, the James Gang rode into Richmond, Missouri, on May 22, 1867, whooping, hollering, and shooting their pistols into the air. As the townsfolk scattered, six members of the gang—Jesse and Frank, Cole, James White, and Jim and Bob Younger—broke down the bank's front door. They grabbed nearly $4,000 in cash and stuffed it into a wheat sack.

By this time, some of the citizens had figured out what was happening. When the bandits emerged from the building, several people opened fire. Mayor John Shaw, rallying a group of citizens behind him, ran down the street toward the bank. The gang opened fire, and the mayor's body slumped to the ground.

Emboldened by their successful getaway, the outlaws galloped to the city jail, where several ex-Confederates were being held. As they attempted to batter down the door, the fifteen-year-old son of the jailer grabbed a rifle and began shooting at the gang from across the street. The bandits jumped on their horses and rode past the boy, shooting him and leaving him for dead. When the boy's father emerged from the jail and raced to his son's side, they shot him as well.

The town sheriff quickly organized a posse and took off after the murderers, catching up with them at sundown. During a wild shootout, several gang members were identified before they had a chance to slip away under cover of darkness. The posse tracked down one member, Payne Jones, at his ranch house. Jones emerged with six-guns blazing, shooting a young girl and a posse member before he himself was shot and killed.

Next, the posse tracked Richard Burns to a farmhouse near Richmond. Several vigilantes took him to a large tree and, with torches flaring, hanged him. Andy Maguire and Tom Little, also identified as members of the gang, were likewise caught and hanged. But no one was willing to go up against two of the most feared gunmen in the West. No one would face the blazing guns and quick tempers of the James brothers.

RAIDING THE RAILS

By the early 1870s, Frank and Jesse were growing weary of robbing banks, so they decided to hit the rails. Trains often carried large amounts of cash destined for banks and businesses throughout the area. Frank had ridden the rails several times in his younger days. His tales of tens of thousands of dollars in gold on board the Pacific Express soon caught the attention of the other gang members.

So on July 21, 1873, the James Gang arrived outside Adair, Iowa, and began removing a section of track leading to town. When the

An engraving of a railroad robbery in the West. The Jameses carried off a lot of loot from such raids but badly botched many as well.

Pacific Express came roaring around the bend, the engineer, John Rafferty, saw the break in the tracks and threw the engine into reverse.

Too late! As the great puffing engine reached the break in the tracks, it derailed, tumbling onto its side like a giant dinosaur and killing the engineer.

The gang members suddenly charged out of the nearby woods and galloped up to the baggage car, pointing their guns at the startled clerks and demanding that they open the safe. There they found not $100,000 in gold but $2,000 in federal reserve notes. The gold that had been scheduled for shipment had gone out on the train before, some four hours earlier.

Word of the bold attack spread like wildfire. Soon, every lawman in the territory was after the James Gang—including agents of the famed Pinkerton Detective Agency. (Jesse had an almost obsessive hatred for the agency's founder, Allan Pinkerton. According to some accounts, Pinkerton agents had wounded the James's mother and killed their half-brother during a shootout with the outlaws.) But that didn't slow down the James Gang. On July 7, 1875, the outlaws hopped aboard a Missouri Pacific Railroad engine and leveled their guns on the engineer, who promptly brought the train to a stop. Cole then broke into the safe, and Jesse removed more than $75,000.

As the gang members climbed onto their horses, Jesse called out to guard John Bushnell. "If you see any of the Pinkertons, tell 'em to come and get us."[3]

THE GANG'S UNDOING

Following their largest strike to date, the gang decided it was time for an even bigger haul—the sprawling First National Bank in Northfield, Minnesota, one of the wealthiest banks in the Midwest. Although it was far distant from the gang's usual haunts, it was alleged to have as much as $200,000 on hand. Northfield was a town filled with hard-working,

The First National Bank as it looked when the James Gang robbed it.

frugal citizens. In addition, two of the bank's main stockholders were Ben Butler and W. A. Ames, both former Union officers during the Civil War. That was all the James brothers needed to hear. In August 1876, the gang set out, reaching Northfield on September 7.

At 2 P.M., Frank, Bill Chadwell (alias William Stiles), and Jim Younger rode to one end of town, where they guarded the gang's escape route. Meanwhile, Jesse, Charlie Pitts, and Bob Younger entered the First National Bank. Cole Younger and Clell Miller waited outside, holding the horses. Then the trouble began.

When J. S. Allen, a local merchant, saw the two strangers standing outside the bank, he walked over to see what was happening. Miller grabbed Allen's arm and warned him to keep his mouth shut. But Allen broke free and ran down the street, yelling, "They're robbing the bank! They're robbing the bank! Get your guns, boys! They're robbing the bank!"[4]

Inside, Jesse was having trouble convincing bank cashier Joseph Heywood to open the vault. Heywood insisted there was a time lock on it and that the lock wouldn't open until the next morning. Suddenly the bandits heard shooting in the street.

"The game's up!" Pitts called, peering out the window. "Pull out or they'll kill us all!"[5]

Before the three ran out into the street, one of them turned and fired at Heywood, who took a bullet to the head and fell dead to the floor.

Outside, a bullet from a nearby rifle hit Cole Younger's shoulder. Another punctured Bill Chadwell's heart. Clell Miller was shot from his horse and lay dead. Bob Younger, searching desperately for an escape route through the barricade, was shot, perhaps through the hand.

Mug shots of two of the Younger brothers, Cole (left) and Jim.

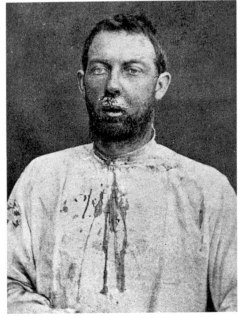

By now, dozens of citizens had grabbed their guns and were shooting at the outlaws. One bullet struck Charlie Pitts. Another hit Jim Younger. A third pierced Cole. The gang was slowly being cut to pieces.

Finally Jesse motioned to make a break. Bob Younger, who had been shot off his horse, scurried to the center of the street as the other gang members spurred their horses on.

"My God, boys, you're not deserting me!" he called out. "I'm shot!"[6]

Cole, hearing his brother's plea, turned back, pulled Bob onto his horse, and together the bloodied and battered gang broke through the barricade and past the heavy fire.

When they had ridden several miles outside of town, they stopped to rest for a few minutes. According to some accounts, Jesse demanded that the gang abandon the wounded Younger. When Cole refused, the James brothers left them both behind. In any event, the gang split up. Jesse and Frank, the only two bandits in the gang who had escaped uninjured, rode off in one direction, while the rest of the gang headed off in another.

The Youngers, slowed down by their wounds, left an easy trail for the pursuing posse. Two weeks later, they were captured in a swamp outside Madelia, Minnesota. Charlie Pitts was dead.

"I KILLED JESSE JAMES!"

Meanwhile, the James brothers, now notorious from one end of the country to the other, found themselves the object of the largest manhunt in the history of the Old West. They made their way to Alabama, where they continued their outlaw ways, before finally returning to Missouri, where they killed a conductor on the Chicago, Rock Island, and Pacific Railroad at Winston. The governor of Missouri, Thomas T. Crittenden, posted a reward of $5,000 apiece for the capture and conviction of Frank and Jesse James. It would prove to be the final blow.

Following one last raid on a train outside Glendale, Missouri, Jesse returned to his home in St. Joseph. There, on the morning of April 3, 1882, he called two former gang members—Charles and Robert Ford—to meet with him to plan the robbery of the Platte County Bank. As Jesse rose to straighten a small picture on the wall, Robert, who knew all too well of the reward, pulled a pistol and pointed it squarely at Jesse's back. Then, at a distance of about 4 feet (1.2 meters), he emptied his revolver into the bandit. Jesse spun on his heels to glare at his traitorous assassin, then slumped to the floor, dead.

The Fords raced from the house, all the while Robert shouting, "I killed him! I killed Jesse James!"[7]

Within minutes, the Fords wired Governor Crittenden that the most wanted man in America was dead. Robert demanded his reward, and, true to his word, Crittenden had money sent to him—although no one is certain it was the full amount promised.

Following a brief funeral attended by hundreds of curious on-lookers, Jesse's mother took her son's casket back with her to the family farm. There, Jesse was laid to rest. A simple white marble headstone was placed over his grave.

JESSE W. JAMES
DIED APRIL 3, 1882
AGED 34 YEARS, 6 MONTHS, 28 DAYS
MURDERED BY A TRAITOR AND A COWARD
WHOSE NAME IS NOT WORTHY TO
APPEAR HERE

Five months after his brother's murder, on October 5, 1882, Frank James—with nothing left to live for—surrendered to authorities. He was tried several times and eventually acquitted of his crimes. He spent the rest of his life working peacefully on the family farm and died in bed on February 18, 1915, thus bringing to an end one of the most infamous reigns of terror in the Old West.

WANTED

BILLY THE KID

Hollywood made many pictures about Billy the Kid. This shot comes from an early one and shows a handsome, innocent-looking Billy torn between love and the law.

Billy the Kid, one of the most notorious outlaws in the Old West, was born Henry McCarty in New York City on November 23, 1859. Historians disagree over the facts of Billy's life, particularly his early years. According to most accounts, Billy's father Patrick died young, and Billy and his mother Catherine eventually found their way to Santa Fe, New Mexico, where she married William Henry Harrison Antrim. They moved with Billy and his brother (or half-brother), Joseph, to Silver City, where Antrim took a job as a miner and Catherine ran a small boarding house.

In 1874, Billy's mother died, leaving her two sons in Antrim's care. But Antrim and Billy did not get along, so at the age of fifteen, Billy left home. He drifted throughout New Mexico and Arizona in search of odd jobs. During this period he learned to shoot and ride better than most men. He also was arrested for the first time—for stealing clothes from Chinese immigrants.

In Arizona or New Mexico (accounts vary), Billy crossed paths with a blacksmith, Frank P. Cahill. An argument broke out, and Cahill, known for his quick temper, slapped the youngster in the face and threw him to the floor. As the stocky Cahill reached down to grab the boy, Billy drew his six-shooter and fired a single shot through Cahill's heart.

Following the shooting, Billy fled to Lincoln, New Mexico, where he met rancher and shopkeeper John Tunstall. The two quickly hit it off, and Tunstall hired Billy, who soon grew to regard the rancher as the "father" he had never had. Tunstall called Billy "the Kid" because of his boyish face and slim figure.

VENGEANCE

On February 18, 1878, while riding down a deserted road with Billy and several other ranch hands trailing behind, Tunstall ran into a group of gunmen who had been hired by neighboring ranchers L. G. Murphy and J. J. Dolan. The men got into an argument, and Jesse Evans shot Tunstall in the chest. As the rancher fell to the ground, another member of the gang, Billy Morton—who earlier in the day had told his companions, "Hurry up, boys, my knife is sharp and I feel like scalping someone"—fired a fatal bullet into Tunstall's head.[1]

Billy was heartbroken over the death of Tunstall, the only man he had ever cared about. Visiting the back room of the Tunstall store, where the dead man's body had been laid out, Billy, half in tears, vowed, "I'll get some of them before I die."[2] And, soon enough, he did just that.

Dick Brewer, a law-abiding citizen who would later be named special constable, formed a posse, called the Regulators, to go after Tunstall's murderers. Included were Alexander McSween, who was Tunstall's friend and attorney, and Billy.

After tracking the gunmen for several days, the posse overtook two members of Dolan's gang, Billy Morton and Frank Baker, and arrested them to stand trial back in Lincoln. But Morton had doubts that he would ever make it back to town. "The constable himself said he was sorry we gave up," Morton wrote later, "as he had not wished to take us alive."[3]

*The real
Billy the Kid.*

At dusk the next evening, Morton managed to grab a pistol from the arresting deputy and shot the lawman dead. Then he and Baker made a break for freedom. Billy took off after them, caught them, and killed them both.

OUTLAW STATUS

Billy returned to Lincoln and went to work for McSween, where he became involved in a legal battle that would change his life. On March 9, New Mexico Governor Samuel B. Axtell arrived in Lincoln to investigate the growing feud between the Regulators and the Dolans. In an attempt to bring peace to the area, Axtell declared Sheriff William Brady to be the only legally appointed law officer in the county. He canceled the legal standing of the Regulators and ordered the men who had arrested and killed Morton and Baker to be apprehended to stand trial. Learning that Sheriff Brady was armed with a warrant for their arrest, McSween, Billy, and the rest of the Regulators took to the hills.

Throughout the month of March, the Regulators lay low. They met several times to discuss their situation, and each time several members of the outlaw band voiced their desire to rid the county of Sheriff Brady once and for all. Finally, on the night of March 31, the Regulators prepared to act.

The next morning, as Sheriff Brady walked down the street toward the courthouse, a group of concealed gunmen rose from behind a wall, pointed their Winchester rifles at the lawman, and opened fire. Brady returned fire and a swarm of bullets swept the street. When the shooting was over, Brady lay dead. Two of the Regulators, Billy the Kid and Jim French, had been wounded but managed to escape.

Before long, the entire county buzzed with the news. Billy the Kid and his friends were no longer citizens in search of justice. They were cold-blooded murderers.

SHOOTOUT AT BLAZER'S MILL

When Billy heard the rumor that Andrew "Buckshot" Roberts, another Dolan gang member, was in the area, he once again set out with the Regulators. The vigilantes caught up with Roberts in April 1878 at Blazer's Mill, New Mexico, and posse member Frank Coe went out to try to talk him into surrendering. Roberts answered, "No, never alive. The Kid is with you and he will kill me on sight."[4]

Roberts raised his Winchester rifle and began firing. One bullet ricocheted off the pistol belt of one of the Regulators, Charlie Bowdre, and into Coe's right hand. Bowdre returned fire, sending a bullet into Roberts's abdomen. Roberts, seriously wounded, managed to stumble back through the doorway of Dr. Blazer's house, firing from the hip as he retreated. One shot lodged in the lung of posse member John Middleton. Another hit the barrel of Doc Scurlock's pistol and deflected down his leg, "burning him like a hot iron."[5] A third whizzed past Billy's head.

As the Kid slipped in between the house and a wagon, Roberts took a shot at him, just shaving his arm.

While the Regulators peppered the building with bullets, Billy carefully counted the shots from Roberts's rifle. When the weapon was finally empty, he dashed to the porch and shoved his own Winchester through the door. When Roberts saw the barrel of Billy's gun, he shoved the muzzle of his own carbine into Billy's stomach, knocking the Kid breathless and deflecting the shot into the door jamb. Roberts then dropped the gun, ran back into Blazer's office, and grabbed a loaded Springfield from the wall.

Meanwhile, Regulators leader Dick Brewer took cover behind some logs near the sawmill and opened fire, with one bullet slamming into the wall behind Roberts. Roberts noticed the smoke from Brewer's rifle rising from the log pile and patiently aimed his rifle at the spot.

Finally, Brewer's head appeared. Roberts fired the big Springfield at Brewer, killing him instantly.

With Brewer dead, the posse members decided to wait for Roberts's stomach wound to take its toll. Sure enough, they found Roberts dead the next morning.

When news of the battle reached Lincoln, the entire town began buzzing over the gunfight. The legend of Billy the Kid, the young gunfighter who knew no fear, spread like wildfire.

With Morton, Baker, and Roberts dead, Billy now set out after the other members of the Dolan gang. One killing followed another as the feud between the Regulators and the Dolans continued. It came to a head on the night of July 15, 1878, when Billy and several others took refuge for the night in a large mansion in Lincoln. Outside, George Peppin, the town's new sheriff, and forty of the area's most noted gunfighters demanded Billy's surrender for his part in the killings. When Billy refused, the sheriff's men set fire to the house.

With the old wooden building burning, McSween made a break for safety. He burst through the doorway, only to be shot and killed instantly. Harvey Morris, a law student working for McSween, emerged next from the fiery inferno and was likewise killed. Billy sent a barrage of shots into the night, killing deputies Robert Beckwith and John Jones. Then the young outlaw shouted to his comrades, "Come on!"[6] Billy jumped over Beckwith's body, followed closely by his companions, and, with six-guns blazing, escaped to freedom.

ON THE RUN

During the next two years, the fighting continued at a frantic pace. By now, the steely-eyed youth with receding chin and buck teeth had become the most sought after outlaw in the territory. So vicious were the murders committed by the Regulators and the Dolans, the dispute soon came to be known as the Lincoln County War.

In a saloon shootout with Billy the Kid,
the other guy never had a chance.

When President Rutherford B. Hayes named Lew Wallace as the new territorial governor, Billy volunteered to surrender if the governor would offer him a pardon in exchange for testifying against the other members of the Regulators. Wallace personally guaranteed Billy's freedom. But as the trial date grew close, Billy had second thoughts. In early January 1880, he broke out of jail, stole a horse, and rode to Fort Sumner, where he ran into Texan Joe Grant, a drunken gunfighter who had bragged that he would kill Billy the Kid the first time he laid eyes on him.

Billy, too, listened to Grant's bragging, then asked to see the gunman's expensive pistol. Grant, not recognizing the youth as the most notorious outlaw in the West, slid the gun out of its holster and handed it to Billy.

While Grant was momentarily distracted, Billy slipped three shells out of the pistol's cylinder and handed the weapon back to Grant. A short time later, Billy identified himself as the Kid that Grant had been seeking and called the gunman out into the street. In the shootout that followed, Grant drew smooth and fast, but when he pulled the trigger, the hammer echoed blankly against the empty chamber. While Grant stood stunned, Billy calmly drew his pistol, aimed, and fired.

By now, Billy's reputation as a ruthless killer had spread throughout the country. Dozens of gunmen were out looking for him. All were determined to make a name for themselves by outdrawing one of the fastest guns in the West. Governor Wallace was looking for Billy, too. But this time he wasn't about to offer the gunman a deal. This time he wanted him brought to justice—dead or alive.

Wallace appointed Pat Garrett as sheriff of Lincoln County. Garrett, unusually tall at 6 feet 6 inches (198 centimeters), was no stranger to Billy. The two had worked together on a ranch and had played cards and even gotten drunk together in the local saloon. The two might even have become good friends, had Garrett not crossed the line to the opposite side of the law. Now he had just one goal: to bring in Billy the Kid.

Garrett formed a posse of some twenty men and began his relentless pursuit of the Kid. Wherever Billy went, Garrett was only a few steps behind. On December 18, 1880, Garrett received a tip that Billy and his gang were heading for Fort Sumner. The lawman and his deputies set a trap. As the gang rode into view, Garrett opened fire, hitting lead gang member Tom O'Folliard and knocking him from his horse while the rest of the gang turned and fled. Garrett asked O'Folliard where Billy's hideout was, but the wounded man refused to say.

Convinced that he was closing in on the Kid, Garrett spent the next few days in hot pursuit. Finally, on December 21, the lawman caught up with Billy and several members of his gang at a deserted farmhouse near Stinking Springs. Garrett called out for Billy to surrender. Billy and his gang met the demand with a withering storm of bullets. For two days and nights, the siege continued. The gang members, running short of food and water, were in desperate shape. When Charlie Bowdre, Billy's closest friend, walked past an open window, he was shot in the chest and killed.

With Billy's friend gone and several other gang members wounded, the Kid finally decided to surrender. Garrett quickly put Billy in chains and carted him off to Mesilla, New Mexico, where on April 9, 1881, he was tried, convicted, and sentenced to death for murder.

While awaiting execution, Billy was placed under the guard of J. W. Bell and Robert Ollinger, two of Garrett's best deputies. On April 28, while Ollinger was out, Billy asked Bell to help him to the outhouse. Hobbling down the stairs in his chains, Billy suddenly whirled and knocked Bell down with his shoulder. The Kid then managed to get a gun. Some say one was planted in the outhouse. Others say Billy quickly hopped to Garrett's gun room and grabbed a weapon there. When Bell came running in and saw the gun in Billy's hands, he pleaded with him to put it down. "Sorry, Bell," Billy said, and he shot the deputy dead.[7]

Knowing that Ollinger had heard the gunshot and would soon come running, Billy hobbled up the stairs to a second-story balcony overlooking the street. There, with loaded shotgun in hand, he waited patiently for Ollinger, who eventually came scurrying down the street to the jailhouse door.

"Hello, Bob," a calm voice called out. As Ollinger looked up, the Kid cocked both hammers of the shotgun, aimed at Ollinger's head, and calmly pulled the trigger.[8]

Billy hobbled back downstairs, broke out of his shackles, and grabbed several pistols and a Winchester rifle. Then he sneaked out the back door and hopped on a horse that had been tied outside the jail.

When news of what had happened reached Garrett, he was furious. He vowed that he would spend the rest of his life tracking down the man who had killed his two best deputies.

"QUIEN ES?"

On July 14, 1881, Garrett rode out to the old Maxwell ranch on a tip that Billy was holing up there. While an anxious posse waited outside, Garrett moved quietly down the darkened hall to the bedroom.

Billy, who had been visiting a Mexican woman working at the ranch, heard footsteps and called out in Spanish, "*Quien es? Quien es?* [Who's there?]"[9] There are many versions of what happened next. According to one, when no one replied to Billy's question, the outlaw entered the hallway to find himself staring down the gun barrel of his old friend, Pat Garrett. Another story has it that Billy the Kid never even saw Garrett.

Outside, the posse members heard two shots. Thinking that Garrett had been shot and fearing for their own lives, they started mounting up when Garrett came running out the front door.

"I killed the Kid! I killed the Kid!" he yelled.[10]

When the posse members went inside, they found Billy the Kid dead. Garrett's first shot had pierced his heart; the second had flown harmlessly into the wall.

Pat Garrett, the lawman who brought in Billy the Kid. Ironically, Garrett helped contribute to Billy's status as a legendary figure. After Billy's death, he wrote a glorified account of the crimes and capture of "the noted desperado of the Southwest."

By the time the lawmen arrived back in town with the lifeless body of Billy the Kid, rumors began to fly that Garrett had shot the Kid in the back. Despite his insistence that the Kid had drawn first and he had no alternative but to shoot, Garrett was accused of murder and forced to stand trial. The jury found him innocent, and he was set free.

Whether Garrett had shot and killed Billy after the Kid drew on him or shot him in cold blood, no one knows for sure. The man who slew the most notorious outlaw in the Old West eventually retired and bought a small ranch in the mountains, where he himself was shot and killed by an assassin in February 1908.

Meanwhile, Billy—who had died just four months before his twenty-second birthday—lay in a common grave with his two closest friends, Tom O'Folliard and Charlie Bowdre, just outside Fort Sumner, New Mexico. On the gravestone were inscribed the names of the three, the dates that each died, and the word, "Pals."

And on Billy's gun—silenced once and for all—were twenty-one notches, one for each man the Kid had shot and killed during his short but violent time on earth.

WANTED

THE WILD BUNCH (LEFT TO RIGHT): HARRY LONGBAUGH (THE SUNDANCE KID), WILL CARVER, BEN KILPATRICK, HARVEY LOGAN, AND BUTCH CASSIDY.

BUTCH CASSIDY
AND THE
WILD BUNCH

A scene from the popular film "Butch Cassidy and the Sundance Kid."
Stars Paul Newman (left, as Butch Cassidy) and Robert Redford (as
Sundance) portrayed the outlaws as handsome ruffians.

Butch Cassidy and his gang, the Wild Bunch, were the last and most famous of the old-time western robbers. Cassidy himself was not the mean-spirited, cold-hearted killer that so many of his contemporaries were. Rather, he was an intelligent, easy-going man who preferred using his brains over his guns. But he *was* an outlaw: He backed himself up with the lightning-fast draw artist Harry Longbaugh, better known as the Sundance Kid, as well as with Will Carver, Ben Kilpatrick, and Harvey Logan, a deadly killer who vowed never to be taken alive—and ultimately kept his promise.

AN OUTLAW NAMESAKE

Born Robert Leroy Parker in Beaver, Utah, on April 13, 1866, Cassidy borrowed his last name from fellow outlaw Mike Cassidy, from whom he learned to shoot, ride, rob, and rustle (steal) cattle. When Mike Cassidy retired from outlawry, the younger Cassidy took over his gang. Later, he met Bill and Tom McCarty, two brothers with whom he pulled several bank and train robberies.

Robert Leroy Parker, age 17, just before he took the name Cassidy.

One of the things that Cassidy admired most about Tom McCarty was his bizarre sense of humor. Once, while casing the First National Bank of Denver, McCarty approached the bank president.

"Excuse me, sir," he said, "but I just overheard a plot to rob this bank."

The president, momentarily stunned, looked up at McCarty and stammered, "Lord! How did you learn of this plot?"

"I planned it," McCarty replied, then pulled out his Colt .45 and aimed it straight at the president's head. "Put up your hands."[1]

The gang walked away with more than $20,000 from that robbery, adding another $11,000 from a holdup of a bank in Telluride, Colorado. Neither job required the firing of a single shot, which was how Cassidy liked it.

After dividing the loot, Cassidy decided it would be safest to go straight—at least for a while. He worked for several months as a cowboy in Wyoming and even held a job as a butcher in Rock Springs, where he was given the nickname "Butch."

Cassidy got his start in crime rustling cattle. This engraving shows a band of outlaws raiding cattle in Texas.

THE WILD BUNCH

After being released from prison in January 1896 for extorting money from local ranchers, Cassidy headed to Hole-in-the-Wall, Colorado. He had learned about the place—a hideout for America's most desperate outlaws—while in prison.

At Hole-in-the-Wall, Cassidy was greeted by the Logan brothers, Lonnie and Harvey. Harvey was a ruthless killer with a violent temper and piercing black eyes. Also on hand were hardened criminals Bob Meeks and William "Elzy" Lay.

By now, Cassidy had decided to form a gang the likes of which would never again be seen in the Old West. He realized that times were changing. More lawmen and improved telegraph communications made it difficult for outlaws to escape the law—even in the most remote parts of the United States. Cassidy knew that if he were going to make a living from robbery, he would have to do it soon.

He also knew that riding into a town with guns blazing was just plain foolish. So he preached to his fellow outlaws the value of learning ahead of time how many law officers a town had, how strong a vigilante group it boasted, and how much money the local bank had on hand.

On August 13, 1896, after months of careful planning, Cassidy and his gang, the Wild Bunch, decided to test Cassidy's theories. After spending weeks scouting the Montpelier Bank, the gang members successfully robbed it of more than $7,000. Next, they hit a mining camp in Castle Gate, Utah, where Cassidy had once worked. He knew when the payroll money was received and paid out, so the gang members had no trouble timing their strike just right and riding off with as much as $8,000. Before they made their getaway, they cut the telegraph lines so camp officials couldn't wire local lawmen about the robbery.

After lying low for several months, Cassidy and the Wild Bunch, which by now included Harvey Logan, Walt Putney, Tom O'Day, and

Indian Billy Roberts, rode to Belle Fourche, South Dakota. On June 28, 1897, they robbed a local bank of $5,000.

"ALL WE WANT IS THE MONEY"

Following the robbery, the Wild Bunch once again lay low, using their time off to plot their first train holdup. After nearly two years of planning, the gang—which now included the Logan brothers, Elzy Lay, George "Flatnose" Curry, Ben Kilpatrick, Ben Beeson, and the Sundance Kid—sprang into action.

On June 2, 1899, the gang barricaded the narrow trestle at Wilcox, Wyoming, bringing the Union Pacific's Overland Flyer to a screeching halt. While two men leveled their guns on the engineer, the others stood outside the car that carried the money and called for the guard to open the door. "All we want is the money. We won't give you any more trouble, and you can be on your way," Cassidy shouted.[2]

The guard, identified only as Woodcock, recognized Cassidy's voice. "No, I'm sorry, I can't do that," he yelled back.[3] Anticipating the likelihood of just such a problem, Cassidy had brought along a charge of dynamite, which he placed outside the car door. Unfortunately, he knew less about dynamite than he did about human nature. As the bandits dove for cover, the dynamite exploded, sending rubble—and the defiant guard—hurtling through the air. The car split open like a ripe watermelon.

Logan ran up to the guard, who lay dazed and confused but still alive, and pressed the barrel of his gun against the man's head. As he prepared to pull the trigger, Cassidy came up and knocked the gun aside. "A man with that kind of nerve deserves not to be shot," he declared.[4]

Meanwhile, the rest of the gang were scampering up and down the tracks, desperately trying to gather up the more than $30,000 in bank notes and securities blowing in the wind. They had to stop when they heard the whistle of another train right behind the one they had blown up. They suspected that it contained a passenger car full of sheriff's men and a boxcar filled with horses and deputies. And they were right.

Despite the limited success of their first train robbery, news of the Wild Bunch's daring exploit spread throughout the West. Union Pacific officials hired the Pinkerton Detective Agency to bring the robbers to justice. Dozens of other lawmen scoured the countryside, determined to capture the members of the gang.

This photo shows the Pinkerton agents hired to capture the Wild Bunch. From left they are: George Hiatt, T. T. Kelliher, Joe Lefores, H. Davis, Si Funk, and Jeff Carr.

HOLE-IN-THE-WALL

Knowing that lawmen would be looking for them, Cassidy ordered the gang to split up. He, Ben Kilpatrick, and the Sundance Kid—who by now had become Butch Cassidy's closest friend and ally—headed straight for Hole-in-the-Wall. The Logans, Curry, and Lay took off together on a more roundabout route that would eventually lead them back to the same destination.

At Hole-in-the-Wall, Cassidy knew the gang would be safe—not so much because the local lawmen didn't know about the place. They did. More likely, it was because the local ranchers—many of whom had been cattle rustlers and petty thieves themselves—were protective of Cassidy, whom they considered to be one of them.

After more than a year of lying low at Hole-in-the-Wall, Cassidy reorganized the gang and headed off on another train raid. Harvey Logan, Ben Beeson, Sundance, and Ben Kilpatrick were there, along with Kilpatrick's companion, Laura Bullion.

BANK NOTES AND THANKS NOTES

On August 29, 1900, the group stopped the Union Pacific's Train Number 3 at Tipton, Wyoming. Ironically, the same guard, Woodcock, was once again in the mail car and once again refused to open the door.

Cassidy, his patience growing thin, threw up his hands and told the engineer, "You tell that iron-headed Woodcock that if he doesn't open the door this time, we're going to blow him and the whole damned car sky high!"[5]

The engineer finally persuaded Woodcock to open the car door. How much the bandits took is unclear. Some reports suggest it was more than $50,000. Others put the amount at $50.

Next, the gang struck the bank at Winnemucca, Nevada, on September 19, taking in nearly $30,000. Folklore has it that on their way out of town, the members stopped to have their picture taken at the local portrait studio—then sent the photo back to the Winnemucca bank president, thanking him for contributing to their coffers! But the Wild Bunch's arrogance, the legend says, came back to haunt them. Authorities are said to have circulated the photo so that lawmen would be better able to spot the outlaws.

After lying low for nearly a year, the gang decided to pull one more train robbery. The day before the Fourth of July, 1901, Cassidy, Sundance, Logan, Kilpatrick, and Deaf Charley Hanks rode to Wagner, Montana, where they stopped the Great Northern Flyer. This time, Cassidy was more careful. He planted just the right size of dynamite charge beneath the Adams Express car and blew it off the tracks. The gang opened the safe and stole more than $40,000 in bank notes.

THE WILD BUNCH SPLITS

Following that robbery, the Wild Bunch split up for the last time. Ben Kilpatrick and Laura Bullion rode east and were eventually captured. Bullion served only five years in prison. Harvey Logan was finally cornered by a posse and, rather than surrender, took his own life with a single shot through his temple.

Butch Cassidy and the Sundance Kid traveled to Fort Worth, Texas, where Sundance met and fell in love with a woman named Etta Place. Together, the three left for New York, where they spent several weeks eating at the finest restaurants, sleeping in the best hotels, and posing for photographs in their finest formal attire. Then they left for the South American country of Bolivia, where they disguised themselves as mine workers.

In time, Etta grew tired of life on the run and returned to the states, where she changed her name and disappeared into obscurity.

The Sundance Kid and Etta Place in one of the photos they had taken in New York City.

GRINGO BANDITS

Meanwhile, Butch and Sundance, running short on cash, returned to robbery. They quickly built a reputation with the South American authorities, called *federales,* as the gringo (American) bandits who had to be stopped. Finally, they robbed a Bolivian payroll in Aramayo and were trapped in the tiny village of San Vincente by government troops. Some say the year was 1908; others, 1909 or 1911.

What happened next is equally unclear. Some historians say that both Cassidy and Sundance were slaughtered, each riddled with dozens of bullets and left to rot beneath the blazing Bolivian sun. Others believe that Sundance was killed by *federales,* and Cassidy, rather than surrender to the soldiers, put his gun to his temple and pulled the trigger.

Still another story has it that Sundance was wounded in a vicious crossfire with the *federales.* Just before he died, he gave Cassidy a letter to give to Etta Place. Under cover of darkness, Cassidy escaped and returned to the states. According to this account, Cassidy ended up in Utah, the place of his birth. One day a gas station attendant from nearby Baggs, Wyoming, claimed that a shiny black sedan had pulled in to fill up. The man in the back seat had pulled his hat down covering his face, but the attendant was sure he recognized him as Butch Cassidy. When the car pulled out, the attendant jumped in his old truck and followed at a safe distance. When the limousine turned off the main road toward a dead-end canyon, the man slipped his truck behind some brush, where he waited until—sure enough—the black sedan came bouncing past on its way back out. When it seemed safe, the attendant drove up into the canyon, following the sedan's tracks in the red southwestern clay.

There he came across a half-hidden rocky overhang beneath which was a freshly dug hole—just deep enough to hold a fortune in stolen money.

Exactly which one of these stories is true may never be known. What *is* clear is that Butch Cassidy and the Sundance Kid set out to form the last great outlaw gang of the Old West. At this they succeeded. And, in the process, they created one of the most enduring and mysterious legends of the Old West.

As this behind-the-scenes shot of the filming of a Hollywood western shows, a lot of work went into creating the images we have of the American West. Although these images are exciting, they often bear little resemblance to what we know about the West and its outlaws.

AFTERWORD

Neither the James Brothers, nor Billy the Kid, nor Butch Cassidy paid for their crimes in the traditional sense of serving a long prison term. Of the group, only Frank James and Billy the Kid stood trial for their careers of brutality. Frank James was acquitted. Billy escaped.

Does this mean that these outlaws of the American West got away with their crimes? Consider the facts of their lives. With every crime he committed, each man was forced to run from the law. And as the crimes accumulated, and the lawmen became more numerous, the hiding places became fewer. Butch Cassidy and the Sundance Kid were driven to seek refuge in a country thousands of miles from their own—and were still hunted down.

With every bullet he fired, each man's choices became fewer. With every crime, his world narrowed. Finally, Jesse James, Billy the Kid, Butch and Sundance had backed themselves into corners where they could do only one thing: die. Though each of these men has gone down in history as someone who lived *outside* the law, the entire world became, in the end, his prison.

NOTES

FOREWORD

The New Prairie Gazette (Denver, 1922), p. 3.

CHAPTER ONE

1. *The Wild West* (New York: Time-Life Books, 1993), p. 138.
2. Ibid, p. 174.
3. Ibid, p. 182.
4. Ibid.
5. Ibid, p. 183.
6. Ibid., p. 140.
7. Nash, *Encyclopedia of Western Lawmen & Outlaws*, p. 186.

CHAPTER TWO

1. Robert M. Utley, *Billy the Kid*
   (Lincoln: University of Nebraska Press, 1989), p. 45.
2. Ibid, p. 47.
3. Ibid, p. 57.
4. Ibid, p. 72.
5. Ibid.
6. Nash, *Encyclopedia of Western Lawmen & Outlaws*, p. 41.

7. Ibid, p. 44.
8. Ibid.
9. Ibid.
10. Ibid.

CHAPTER THREE

1. Nash, *Encyclopedia of Western Lawmen & Outlaws*, p. 67.
2. Richard and Judy Dockrey Young, eds., *Outlaw Tales* (Little Rock, AR: August House Publishers, 1992), p. 170.
3. Ibid.
4. Nash, *Encyclopedia of Western Lawmen & Outlaws*, p. 67.
5. Ibid.

FURTHER READING

Green, Carl R., and William R. Sanford. *Billy the Kid*. Hillside, NJ: Enslow, 1992.

————. *Jesse James*. Hillside, NJ: Enslow, 1992.

Josephy, Alvin M., Jr., ed. *American Heritage History of the American West*. New York: American Heritage, 1982.

McCarty, Lea F. *Gunfighters*. Tempe, AZ: Smith-South Western, Inc., 1992.

Nash, Jay Robert. *Encyclopedia of Western Lawmen & Outlaws*. New York: Paragon House, 1992.

Sifakis, Stewart. *Who Was Who in the Civil War*. New York: Facts On File Publications, 1988.

Stiles, T. J. *Jesse James*. New York: Chelsea House, 1993.

Utley, Robert M. *Billy the Kid*. Lincoln: University of Nebraska Press, 1989.

The Wild West. New York: Time-Life Books, 1993.

Young, Richard, and Judy Dockrey, eds. *Outlaw Tales*. Little Rock, AR: August House Publishers, 1992.

INDEX